PAPER *Christmas*

First published in Great Britain 2018

Search Press Limited
Wellwood, North Farm Road,
Tunbridge Wells, Kent TN2 3DR

Text copyright © Emily Dawe 2018
Photographs by Paul Bricknell at Search Press Studio;
and Fiona Murray: pages 1, 2–3, 6–7, 16–17 (background
image), 18 (top right), 21, 25, 28 (bottom left), 29, 34–35,
41, 42–43 (background image), 47, 48 (bottom left), 51,
54–55, 59, 63, 69 (bottom left), 70–71 (background image);
76–77, 81, 84–85 (bottom image across spread), 88 (centre
right), 89, 94 (bottom right) and 95.

Photographs and design copyright © Search Press Ltd 2018

ISBN: 978-1-78221-558-5

Suppliers

For details of suppliers, please visit the Search Press
website: www.searchpress.com

You are invited to visit the author's website:
www.emilydawe.com

Printed in China through Asia Pacific Offset

Dedication

I'd like to dedicate this book to my mum and dad. If it
wasn't for their never-ending support and patience,
through years of letting me be creative (taking over our
entire home with my artwork – glue, glitter and paint
everywhere) I wouldn't be lucky enough to be here,
publishing my first book.

Acknowledgements

Thank you to Beth Harwood, Roz Dace and the fantastic
team at Search Press for believing in me. Thank you
to my two wonderful photographers, Paul Bricknell
and Fiona Murray – those endless cups of tea got us
through! – and to Emmeline, for her modelling debut and
invaluable help on the shoot.

Many thanks to the team at Cricut: I really put that
machine to the test! Thank you to Karina at Plastikote
for the spray paints, and to Lynne at Papermash for the
gorgeous leather twine. Thank you to Shelley for letting
us take over your home with bags and boxes of makes
and Christmas props.

And finally, thank you to my husband Cameron, for
being my constant support through this entire process.
My sounding board, my creative muse, my favourite.
The house can go back to normal now...

PAPER *Christmas*

16 papercrafting projects for the festive season

EMILY DAWE

SEARCH PRESS

Contents

GIFT-GIVING 16

Christmas tree cards
18

Heat-embossed
Christmas card
22

Paper feather tags
26

Gift tags
30

Marbled wrapping
paper
36

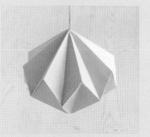

INTRODUCTION

There is something rather magical during the build up to Christmas – it's unlike any other time of the year. Our attention turns to the home and making it as inviting and fabulously festive as possible. So what better time is there to create something handmade? I've created *Paper Christmas*, sixteen beautiful projects that I hope will inspire you and get those creative juices flowing.

Paper is such a versatile material: it can be folded, curled, scored, twisted, heated, embellished, ripped, snipped and dipped, which is why I love working with it so much.

My projects are set to inspire you, so please don't worry if you don't have the exact papers or tools. Use my creations, and the variations at the end of the projects, as springboards for your own uniquely wonderful designs.

Paper Christmas is split into three sections: 'Gift-giving', where you will find inspiration on creating your own cards, gift tags and marbled gift wrap; 'Deck the halls', which includes origami decorations, mini bunting and angels made from old paperback books; and finally, there is 'Festive fun' where I have featured everything from a giant snowflake table runner to sweetie favour cones, Advent houses, and party hats so that you can see in the New Year in style.

There are projects ideal for children and complete beginners through to more intricate projects to develop your skills further. Whether you relish a traditional Christmas or prefer something a little more contemporary and chic for your home, there is something for everyone in *Paper Christmas*.

What are you waiting for? Let's get fun, festive and fabulous with paper. Just turn the page...

PAPERS

Ah, paper! Without it, this book wouldn't even exist. Tissue, origami, handmade, wrapping, cartridge, textured, glittered, heavyweight, banana, recycled, coated, uncoated, silk, matt, gloss... there's a treasure trove of different varieties of paper available, each boasting wonderful and unique qualities for your crafting needs. This is what makes papercrafting so exciting; there is an abundance of choice and endless possibilities.

Paper sizes

Paper comes in a variety of sizes. The standard papers I've used most frequently throughout this book are: 297 x 210 (11¾ x 8¼in) referred to as A4 in the UK; 420 x 297mm (16½ x 11¾in), or A3; and 594 x 420mm (23½ x 16½in), or A2. In the US, letter or legal paper sizes are usually 279 x 216mm (11 x 8½in) or 356 x 216mm (14 x 8½in).

Paper weights

Paper weight is measured by gsm – grams per square metre – or by pounds per ream. The higher the gsm or weight per ream in lbs, the heavier the paper – for example, a standard sheet of copier paper is usually 80gsm (54lbs); good-quality writing paper falls at about 100 or 120gsm (68 to 81lbs); and leaflets can be printed on papers from 130 to 150gsm (88 to 101lbs).

Paper types

There is a huge array of different types of paper available to the papercrafter, each one better suited to a certain function or style of craft. Below, I have detailed some of the 'specialist' papers I have used in *Paper Christmas*:

Origami papers   Available in often strong, vivid colours and patterns, origami papers tend to be thin due to the need to be folded – about 60gsm (41lbs). However, thicker variations are used to make sturdier forms. They are available in different sizes, but mostly commonly pre-cut squares.

Wrapping paper   With so many styles, sizes, weights and textures it really comes down to personal taste when choosing a wrapping paper to work with. The great thing is that it's so readily available. Thin varieties can work well as origami papers, and you can't beat brown kraft paper for wrapping gifts.

Card blanks   Available in a myriad sizes, card blanks are sold flat, with a pre-formed crease along the centre, and come in all sorts of colours, shapes and textures. A greeting card needs to be strong enough to stand up, so card blanks are usually about 300gsm (203lbs).

Cartridge paper   This is a higher quality paper (about 180gsm or 121lbs) often used by artists and illustrators. The texture of the paper is slightly rough, and when compared to standard copier paper, it has a much warmer tone to it.

Watercolour paper   This is usually a heavier weight of paper. It has an irregular, textured surface, making it ideal for paint but also beautiful when left plain. It is available as 'hot press', which has a smooth hard finish, and 'cold press'. Cold press is the popular choice for beginners as it is more textured and more versatile for both detailed pieces and washes of colour.

Opposite: a selection of plain, patterned and glittered papers, all of which are perfect for Christmas papercrafting.

Working with the grain

Did you know every piece of paper has a grain, much like wood does? This is an important factor to consider when tearing it – it will tear much more easily along the grain – and using paper for some specific crafts. For example, if you are folding paper to make a book, it's essential that the grain of the paper runs in the same direction as the spine, otherwise the book will never sit flat.

It's easy to work out which way the grain runs. Take either end of a piece of paper and bring your hands together in the middle. Then rotate the paper and repeat the process. You will notice that one way feels much easier to fold, which indicates the direction of the grain.

Above, working with the grain of the paper:
a) folding the paper with the grain;
b) folding the paper against the grain.

From top left, self-healing cutting mat; hot-glue gun and sticks; washi tapes; cocktail sticks; double-sided tape; glue stick; PVA glue; craft knife (Stanley knife); decorative edging scissors, small craft scissors; scoring tool; tweezers; miniature pegs; dusting brush; black fineliner pen; gold pen; propelling pencil; paintbrush.

MATERIALS AND TOOLS

Every crafter needs an essential tool kit to aid them when creating beautiful projects. These are usually items that you may already have lying around the house, or tucked away in a drawer. I recommend investing in a few good quality tools, things like scissors and glue, as these essentials will last a long time. Quality items will give you quality results.

Papercrafting tools

A self-healing **cutting mat** will protect your work surface from cuts, glue and paint. You can also use the printed grid as a guide when measuring, and when lining up a ruler for cutting.

I have used various types of **glue** in *Paper Christmas* – each glue has its pros and cons. A **glue stick** is ideal for sticking paper to paper as it's not a very wet glue so it won't warp the paper. It is not especially strong, so it is less suitable for sticking papers of considerable weight. PVA glue is a better choice for making projects sturdier – for example, the Advent houses on pages 72–77. Use a **hot-glue gun** to stick different, or weighty, materials together – for example, when constructing the wreath on pages 86–89. For this project, a hot-glue gun may prove essential.

Much like glues, tapes also come in various guises. **Washi tape** is low-tack, much like masking tape, but it's far prettier! Washi tape is often used to decorate projects or to stick pictures to the wall – it's a tape that demands to be seen! **Double-sided tape** is a must if you care about neat gift-wrapping – no shiny tape in sight! It's also my tape of choice for sticking papers together, especially when overlapping them (see: Party hats, pages 90–95).

A **ruler** is essential for measuring and cutting straight lines. Choose a **transparent ruler** when you need to see the position of the paper underneath; if you are using a **craft knife**, however, opt for a **metal ruler** with a cork base to prevent both the ruler – and the knife – slipping.

When using a **pencil**, make sure it's always kept sharp. Alternatively, use a propelling pencil to make accurate lines. A black **fineliner pen** is a great addition to your kit and is perfect for adding tiny, emphatic details.

No Christmas book would be complete without a project using a **gold pen**! Go for the type that you have to shake, as they give the best metallic finish.

Other nifty items I used in *Paper Christmas* include **tweezers** (for positioning minute pieces of paper); miniature **pegs** for holding paper together as the glue adheres; **cocktail sticks** for applying glue to tiny pieces of paper; a **scoring tool** for achieving neat, crisp creases; and **paintbrushes** for applying glue or gilding size.

THREADS, TWINES, RIBBONS, POMPOMS AND BAUBLES

Red and white **baker's twine** is a classic choice for Christmas, for both craft projects and gift-wrapping. Baker's twine is available in a variety of colours, including a more contemporary black and white, and metallic.

Ribbon is the finishing flourish when gift-wrapping, whether you opt for matching or co-ordinating colours. They come in a variety of finishes, such as satin (shiny) and grosgrain (textured, but with a tendency to fray). For the wow factor, invest in some wired ribbon, which can be bent and shaped to create the most perfect, upright bow.

Leather twine makes a stylish alternative to ribbon or twine. It's ideal for use on baubles and tree trims (like my heat-embossed miniature frames, page 24), and as the ties on a party hat (see pages 90–95)

Embroidery skeins aren't just for sewing! A skein is made up of six threads, which can be pulled apart to create thinner strands. Use embroidery threads to string up decorations or tiny bunting, or attach the thread as the legs and feet on your paper bird trims (see pages 52–55).

Baker's twine in black and white, red and white and navy and gold; satin and grosgrain ribbons in mauve and red; wool pompoms; white embroidery thread; gold and silver leather twine; felt pompoms; bauble; embroidery skeins.

Wool **pompoms** are easily made using a pompom maker or using two pieces of circular cardboard – the old-fashioned way. These, along with felt pompoms, are used to decorate the party hats (see pages 90–95).

Old **Christmas baubles** can be revamped and repurposed to create something new. I found that a small bauble made the ideal head for one of my folded-paper angels (see pages 60–63)!

Embellishment tools

It's always lovely to add some decorative finishing touches to your makes. From paper punches to rubber stamps, the items on these two pages will really make a difference to your papercrafting. Of course, no Christmas book would be complete without at least one project involving glitter!

From top left: glitter; luggage label punch; hole punch; star punch; heart punch; rubber letter stamps; Christmas-themed rubber stamps; ink pad.

STAMPS, PUNCHES AND GLITTER

Paper punches are real lifesavers when it comes to cutting out multiple copies of one shape. Star and heart punches appear in a few of my projects, as do a luggage label punch and my trusty hole punch.

Festive-themed **rubber stamps** are ideal for adding decorative motifs in an instant, and you can get ink pads in a spectrum of colours. Letters and numbers are also great for adding a recipient's name to a tag, or to an Advent house (see pages 72–77).

Add sparkle to any project by dipping it in **glitter**! I prefer to tip some glitter into a small bowl, rather than keep it in the tube or packet, as it's much easier to shake off the excess back into the bowl.

CRICUT MACHINE

A Cricut machine is a great investment if you are a keen crafter – it is ideal for cutting out very intricate shapes. This nifty machine works by connecting to a computer program, in which you can design anything your heart desires (or choose from thousands of stock designs). Set a dial to select the material you want to cut: anything from paper, vinyl and cardboard through to chipboard and fabric. Then press 'cut', and *voila*, the machine springs into action and cuts out your shape.

The Cricut machine.

Using the Cricut machine

Position the card onto the mat and press down – the mat is sticky to prevent the card from moving. Load the mat into the machine as far as it will go, using the guides at the side.

Press the button that will start up the rollers, which will take in the mat and engage the cutting element. Then press the flashing Cricut button to start the cut.

Once the cut is finished, take out the mat and carefully pull back the card to reveal the perfectly cut shapes. Use a scraper tool or a knife to lift the shapes from the sticky mat.

The initial on this gift tag has been cut out using the Cricut machine.

TECHNIQUES AND TIPS

Here, I've rounded up a selection of handy techniques and tips that I have learned along the way. Some may seem obvious, but will save you time and give you even better, finished results.

Cutting

 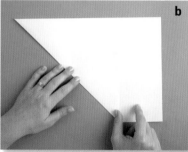 

Cutting a perfect square

It's easy to create a perfect square with a sheet of rectangular paper. Simply pick up one corner and take it over to the opposite edge (**a**). Align the edges of the paper and fold along the diagonal line (**b**). Trim off the excess (**c**).

There you have it – a perfect square!

Using tweezers

It's a good idea to keep a pair of tweezers close to hand when papercrafting, as they can come in very handy.

They're ideal for pulling out cut sections from paper snowflakes (see pages 82–85) or for positioning small or fiddly pieces of paper for gluing.

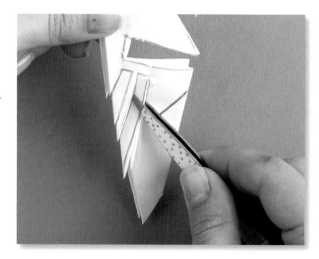

Scoring and creasing

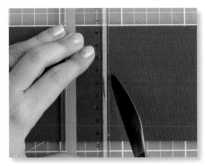

Using a blunt knife for scoring
If you don't have a scoring tool, the blunt edge of a dinner knife does the job just as well.

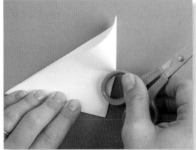

Using scissor handles to crease
Scissors aren't just for cutting – they double up as a clever tool for making your folds lovely and crisp. Simply press the handle along the crease.

Drawing

Using a glue stick as a template
You're most likely to have a glue stick to hand when crafting, so use it as a guide to draw small circles. Otherwise, use a trusty coin.

Sticking and taping

Using double-sided sticky-tape
If you find peeling the backing off double-sided tape difficult, then try this easy trick: before sticking it down, simply fold the end over, sticky side to sticky side (**a**). Lift off the backing to leave a little tab (**b**), perfect for peeling off once you've attached it to paper or card.

Using a cocktail stick to apply glue
A cocktail stick is the ideal-sized tool for applying PVA to small and fiddly pieces of paper.

Gift-giving

Christmas tree cards

Heat-embossed Christmas card

Paper feather tags

Gift tags

Marbled wrapping paper

Christmas tree cards

Rolled-paper Christmas tree card

A very clever, but super-simple, way of creating a stylized Christmas tree design. Simply by making up tubes of paper and cutting them to different lengths, you can create a stunning Christmas tree card in next to no time!

You will need

- ⭐ 125 x 180mm (5 x 7in) kraft (brown) card blank
- ⭐ 150 x 150mm (6 x 6in) patterned paper or wrapping paper
- ⭐ Pencil
- ⭐ Scissors or craft knife
- ⭐ Cutting mat
- ⭐ Ruler
- ⭐ PVA glue and paintbrush

STEP 1
Wrap a 150 x 150mm (6 x 6in) square of patterned paper around your pencil.

STEP 2
Roll the strip of paper tightly around the pencil a few times until you are halfway up the square of paper. Then use a paintbrush to apply a thin line of PVA glue along the edge of the roll.

STEP 3
Roll the paper over the glue and hold in place until the glue has adhered.

Tip
Find the grain of your paper (see page 9) and work with it – it will be easier to curl your paper with the grain than against it.

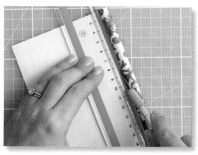

STEP 4

Slide the pencil out of the tube of paper. Then use a craft knife to cut away the excess.

STEP 5

Repeat steps 1 to 4 to make twelve of these paper tubes. Cut the tubes to the lengths as shown on the photograph below:

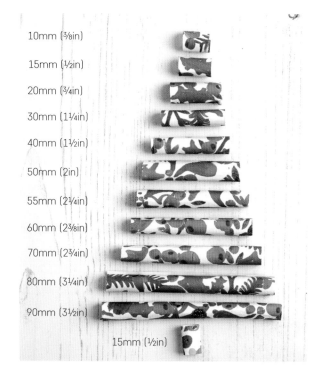

10mm (⅜in)

15mm (½in)

20mm (¾in)

30mm (1¼in)

40mm (1½in)

50mm (2in)

55mm (2¼in)

60mm (2⅜in)

70mm (2¾in)

80mm (3¼in)

90mm (3½in)

15mm (½in)

STEP 6

Arrange the cut tubes in size order on the front of your card blank. Once you are happy with the arrangement, use a paintbrush to apply a line of glue on the back of each tube, where the join is. Finally, stick each tube in place as shown above.

Tip

Instead of making the paper tubes yourself, you can use paper drinking straws cut to size.

Collaged Christmas tree card

Create a beautiful collaged card from patterned and plain papers. The simple but effective design is an ideal way of using up leftover wrapping paper and cards, and can be a fun project to do with the kids.

You can follow the numerical key on the template on page 96 which will help you work out which of the thirteen component shapes should be cut out of each piece of plain or patterned paper – or feel free to experiment.

You will need

- ⭐ 135 x 135mm (5¼ x 5¼in) pale blue card blank
- ⭐ Selection of five different patterned and plain papers
- ⭐ Tracing paper and pencil
- ⭐ Scissors
- ⭐ Glue stick
- ⭐ Template (see page 96)

STEP 1
Trace off the template on page 96.

STEP 2
Take the tracing and place it onto the back of your first piece of paper, Transfer the relevant tree sections onto the paper by drawing over them in pencil (see right).

STEP 3
Cut out the individual parts of the tree from the patterned paper. Continue tracing and cutting out sections of the tree from different papers until you have all the pieces.

STEP 4
Starting with the trunk and lowest sections, arrange the papers as you would like them to appear on the front of your card, working your way up to the top of the tree.

STEP 5
Once you are happy with how your arrangements looks, stick all the pieces in place on your card blank. Start from the trunk and work up.

Your Christmas tree cards.

Heat-embossed Christmas card

Heat embossing sounds more complicated than it really is! The process works by using embossing pens – so you can draw freehand – or an embossing ink pad so you can use a rubber stamp as your design. The embossing powder is then poured on and heated up to create beautiful embossed designs – it's quite magical watching it transform!

You will need

★ 100 x 150mm (4 x 6in) black card blank
★ Tracing paper and pencil
★ Heat embossing pen
★ Gold heat embossing powder
★ Heat gun
★ Gold glittered card
★ Grey embroidery thread
★ Cocktail stick
★ PVA glue and paintbrush
★ Templates (see page 96)

STEP 1
Trace the penguin design from page 96 onto tracing paper.

The heat-embossing kit
From top left: heat gun; heat embossing powders; embossing ink pad; heat embossing pen.

STEP 2
Position the penguin tracing onto the bottom right-hand corner of your black card blank and transfer the mirror image onto the front of the card blank in pencil.

STEP 3
Draw over the whole penguin design with a heat embossing pen.

STEP 4
Tip some gold embossing powder over the design. Don't worry about pouring out too much powder – you can tip any excess back into the pot.

As you tip away the powder, your penguin design will reveal itself!

Tip
If you can see any powder on the card in areas you don't want it, either blow it away or use a cotton bud (a Q-tip) to sweep it off.

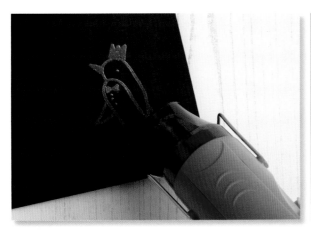

STEP 5
Switch on your heat gun, and position it just above your design. Move the heat gun over the design so that the powder is heated evenly.

STEP 6
Once the powder reaches a certain temperature it will melt and form into a solid. In just a few seconds your design will be completely dry, and the powder won't fall off the card.

STEP 7

Cut a piece of embroidery thread to a length of about 90mm (3½in). Use a cocktail stick to dab PVA glue at either end of the length of thread. Next, stick it, taut, to the card at an angle, as if it's coming from the penguin's flipper.

STEP 8

Cut out the star from the template on page 96 from gold glittered card, and stick it at the top end of the thread, using a glue stick.

STEP 9

Finally, tie a small bow from a separate length of embroidery thread, and trim the tails to a length of about 30–40mm (1¼–1½in). Dab PVA glue to the knot in the bow and adhere it to the first length of thread, just below the star, to complete the card.

Make... a framed miniature picture

If you don't feel confident hand-drawing a much smaller design for heat-embossing, decorative rubber stamps are the ideal solution. Simply press your stamp into an embossing ink pad, then press the stamp onto a piece of black card. Then, as with the main project, tip the powder over, shake off the excess and heat with a heat gun.

You can then trim the card down to the size of a small frame, add a little leather twine (or ribbon) and use them as mini decorations for the tree or to adorn a gift. You could even pop a small one into a tiny envelope and attach to a gift, or write a guest's name on the front of the envelope and use it as a miniature place setting.

Your heat-embossed Christmas card.

Paper feather tags

Make your presents look just as spectacular on the outside as the gift on the inside by trimming them with paper feathers in matching colours and dipping them in glitter. Group three together for larger gifts, or just one or two for smaller presents. You could cut the feathers from matching wrapping paper and write a personal message on the back in gold or silver pen.

You will need

- Thin card or paper in magenta, navy, gold, emerald and olive green
- Scrap card
- Tracing paper and pencil
- Small craft scissors
- Scoring tool
- Cutting mat
- Ruler (optional)
- PVA glue and paintbrush
- Glitter and small bowl
- Ribbon and twine for the presents
- Gold or silver pen (optional)
- Templates (see page 97)

STEP 1

Copy the feather templates from page 97 onto thin card using tracing paper and a pencil. Use the templates to draw a selection of feathers from coloured card or paper.

STEP 2

Cut out around the feather with small, sharp craft scissors.

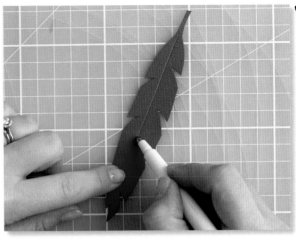

STEP 3

Cut into the finer details of the feathered edges with the craft scissors.

STEP 4

Use a scoring tool to score down the centre of each feather – you can do this freehand on the curved feathers and with a ruler on the straight ones.

Tip

If you don't own a scoring tool, you can use the back of a butter knife or other blunt knife (see page 15) to score down the centre of the feather.

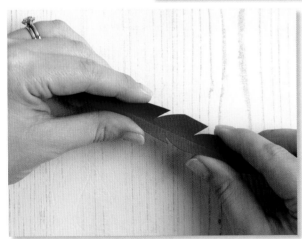

STEP 5

Fold the feathers in half inwards using the scored line.

STEP 6

Apply a little PVA glue to the feather wherever you would like your glitter to adhere. In this example, we're applying glue to the very tip of the feather.

STEP 7
Pour some glitter into a small bowl. Dip the feathers into the glitter so the glued tip is fully coated. Tap off the excess and leave the feathers to dry.

Make... a paper feather garland

Use the feather templates on page 97 to cut out a selection of different-sized feathers from white card, for a cool contemporary feel. Dip them in glue and glitter, as for the tags, and glue them to a length of thin gold ribbon. You may have to use miniature pegs to hold the feathers in place while they are drying. Don't glue the feathers too close together and remember to leave a length of ribbon on either side for tying up.

Once dry, hang your feather garland along a mantel, around the Christmas tree, or in the window.

Your completed paper feather gift tags.

Use miniature pegs to attach your paper feathers to some twine wrapped around a gift.

Gift tags

Tags are an essential part of gift-wrapping – without them you wouldn't know which presents were yours!

Tags can be incredibly simple to make and you don't have to spend a long time on them to achieve something super stylish and guaranteed to make your presents dazzle. We have an array of varied techniques for you to try, from stamping and paper punching to drawing and intricate cutting – and don't forget lots of lovely glitter!

You will need

- ★ Thin card in black, white, and gold glitter
- ★ White paper
- ★ Tracing paper and pencil
- ★ Black fineliner pen
- ★ Glitter
- ★ PVA glue and paintbrush
- ★ Hole punch
- ★ Scissors

- ★ Craft knife
- ★ Cutting mat
- ★ Luggage label, heart and star paper punches
- ★ Rubber stamps – stars, snowflakes and alphabet
- ★ Ink pad
- ★ Baker's twine and ribbon
- ★ Gift tag templates (see pages 96, 98 and 99)

GLITTERED INITIAL TAG

Draw a 65mm (2½in) diameter circle onto white card, or use the template on page 96, and cut it out. Punch a single hole at what will be the top of the tag using a hole punch.

STEP 1
Cut out an initial with a Cricut or a letter punch, or cut out a letter carefully by hand. Glue the initial towards the top-left of the round tag.

STEP 2
Apply some PVA glue diagonally across the tag.

STEP 3a
Shake your glitter over your tag...

STEP 3b
...or dip the tag into a bowl of glitter. Shake any excess back into the bowl and leave your tag to dry.

GLITTERED, LAYERED LUGGAGE TAG

STEP 1

Punch one luggage tag from gold glittered card and one from black card, or use our template on page 96. Place one tag on top of the other and use a hole punch to make a hole through both tags in the same place.

STEP 2

Place the black tag inside a star paper punch, looking underneath to make sure the punch is central on the tag then punch out a star (or use the medium star template on page 96).

STEP 3

Tie the two tags together with baker's twine but don't glue them together – they need to move freely when they are secured to a present.

LITTLE FLAG TAGS

STEP 1

Trace off the little flag tag template on page 98 and cut it out of white card. Punch a hole at the straight end. Apply some PVA glue to the inverted 'V'-end of the tag.

STEP 2

Dip the inverted end of the tag into a bowl of glitter and shake off the excess.

STEP 3

Use a black fineliner pen to hand-write the recipient's name or a festive expression.

Tip

At step 2, don't discard your star – use it for the 'Stars aligned' gift tag project on page 32!

Tip

Layer together a couple of little flag tags on a present and decorate the second tag more simply.

STAMPED TAGS

Trace off the stamped tag template on page 98 and cut out the label shape from white card. Punch a hole at the top and use festive stamps and black ink to decorate the tags as much or as little as you like. If you have alphabet stamps you can write a message or the recipient's name.

These longer luggage tags also make great bookmarks.

BLACK AND GOLD TAGS

Enlarge and cut out a selection of tags from black card, using any of the gift tag templates on pages 96, 98 and 99. Punch a hole in the top of each label. Then, using a gold pen, hand-draw some little festive designs on your labels. These can be little Christmas trees, or even smiling faces on little star-shaped tags.

STARS ALIGNED

Punch out five stars from black card. Line up each star and punch a hole into each one. Thread them together onto a length of baker's twine and wrap the twine around your gift.

BUNTING TAGS
STEP 1
To make a bespoke bunting tag, punch out as many 25mm-(1in-) diameter circles from white paper as there are letters in your recipient's name, plus two extra for little decorations – perhaps some tiny stars.

STEP 2
Use alphabet stamps to spell out the recipient's name, one letter on each circle – try to stamp towards the bottom of each circle. Or, if you prefer, write the person's name letter by letter, neatly, in black fineliner.

STEP 3
Cut a length of baker's twine long enough to wrap twice or three times around your gift. Position the bunting tags in the middle of the length of twine. Fold the circles in half over the twine and glue them in place to secure before wrapping the twine around your gift.

Wrap...

...a tiny model tree to your gift with baker's twine and draw a little car onto the wrap before adding your label, for a truly personal Christmas gift with a twist!

An array of gift tags.

Marbled wrapping paper

You don't need lots of expensive equipment or specialist inks to marble paper. By simply using shaving foam and the coloured paint, ink or food colouring of your choice, you can create beautiful unique patterns in just a few seconds. There's no lengthy drying time, and you can use your marbled papers to wrap presents for loved ones. We've even added a touch of gold leaf for some extra sparkle! The trick is to have fun with the process – sometimes the most beautiful marbled patterns come out when you least expect it.

Tip

As well as using the marbled papers to wrap presents, you can use them to cover notebooks, make gift cards or even frame them – they are works of art!

You will need

- ★ Paper or thin card: this project has been created using 297 x 210mm (11¾ x 8¼in) cartridge paper, but use the most appropriate paper for the size of your present
- ★ Clean, shallow dish such as a plastic litter tray – larger than the piece of paper or card you are marbling
- ★ Shaving foam (not gel)
- ★ Spatula

- ★ Inks, food colouring or paints
- ★ Stick with a fine tip, such as a bamboo skewer or cocktail stick
- ★ Newspaper to protect your work surface
- ★ Kitchen paper
- ★ Old plastic ruler
- ★ Protective gloves
- ★ Miniature peg
- ★ Bow templates (see pages 98–99)

For the gold leaf

- ★ Gilding size (specialist glue)
- ★ Gold gilding leaf
- ★ Small paintbrush
- ★ Soft paintbrush

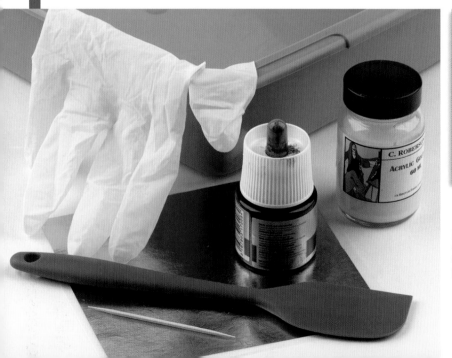

Tip

It's best to use good-quality paper for this marbling project, such as thin card stock or sketchbook paper. Printer paper will give less attractive results.

From top-left: plastic litter tray; gilding size (specialist glue); blue acrylic paint; spatula; cocktail stick; sheet of gold leaf; protective gloves.

STEP 1

First, cover your work surface with newspaper. Give your tray or dish a good clean with some soap and water, then dry it off. Shake up your can of shaving foam and spray a layer of foam into the tray.

STEP 2

Use a plastic spatula to spread the foam out evenly over the tray.

STEP 3

Put on your protective gloves and take up your coloured ink – we've used a vivid blue acrylic ink. Start by adding a few small drops of colour – a little goes a long way. You can always add more.

STEP 4

Use the spatula again to mix the ink into the foam and create beautiful streaks of colour. Work some sections more than others to achieve varied strengths of colour in different areas.

Tip

At step 3 you could add a second ink colour, such as yellow, which will work well with blue to create a vibrant green.

STEP 5

Next, use the point of a cocktail stick or skewer to draw fine patterns into the foam with the ink. This will bring you closer to the marbled effect you're aiming for.

STEP 6

Push your sheet of paper or card into the shaving foam. Press down the paper to smooth out any air bubbles so that the whole sheet will be coated.

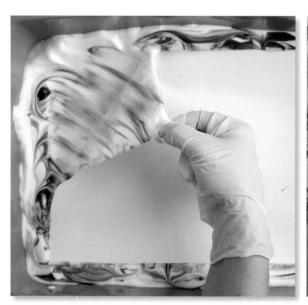

STEP 7

Carefully start to peel away the paper from the shaving foam, starting from one corner. Lay your paper marbled-side up on your newspaper surface – things are about to get really messy!

STEP 8

Scrape an old plastic ruler over the entire surface of the foamy paper. Scrape off all of the foam – either put it back in the tray for later use, or wipe it off the ruler with a sheet of kitchen paper. Then set your sheet of marbled paper aside to dry – it will not take long as shaving foam dries very quickly.

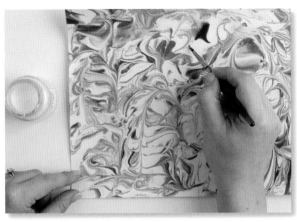

STEP 9

Once your design has dried, apply a little gilding size (specialist gilding glue) with a thin paintbrush. Follow the edges of some of your patterns with the size and leave it for a few minutes until it goes tacky – it will remain tacky and will not dry out.

STEP 10

Rub a small square of gold leaf over your marbled paper so that the gold adheres to the tacky gilding size. Once you've gone over all the areas where the size is, leave to dry.

STEP 11

Take a soft paintbrush and brush over the gold leaf to remove any gold that has not stuck. Little flecks will come away, leaving gold only where the gilding size has been applied. The flecks can also look very effective as part of the design, so you could add a little more of the size and press the gold flecks into it.

The finished design.

Once you are happy with your design, you can then use your papers to wrap presents for that special person in your life. The gold leaf looks really magical when the light hits it. On the next page we use this sheet of marbled paper to create a glamorous bow for a gift.

Marbled gift bow

Creating a matching bow from some left-over marbled paper is easy and will finish off your wrapped present perfectly. Simply trace off our templates on pages 98–99, cut them out and stick them together, and ta-da — you'll have the most beautiful three-dimensional bow!

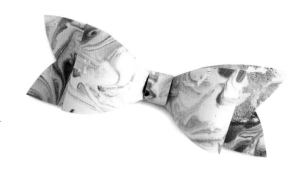

STEP 1
Trace off the three bow templates from pages 98–99 (two bow shapes plus centre band). Next, trace the shapes onto the reverse of your marbled paper. Cut out the three shapes.

STEP 2
Take the first bow shape (the top loop) and bend both wings inwards.

STEP 3
Dab a spot of glue on the centre of the bow and secure the two wings to it. Attach a tiny peg to help stick the two wings in place.

STEP 4
Once the glue has dried, stick the folded bow part to the front of the flat (bottom) bow part.

STEP 5
Finaliy, wrap the centre band around the double bow and glue the two ends together on the reverse.

The finished, wrapped present, complete with matching marble bow.

Deck the halls

Mini bunting

Origami stars

Paper bird trims

Winter tree domes

Diamond decorations

Folded-book angels

Mini bunting

Who doesn't love a bit of bunting? It instantly transforms a room, looks cheery for a party, romantic for a wedding, and magical at Christmas. This mini paper bunting is super easy to make. It does involve a lot of cutting-out, but you can make the lengths as long or short as you like. As well as the traditional pennants bunting, we have templates for stockings, stars and circles to add variety to your decor.

You will need

- ★ Paper or thin card in six different patterns or colours
- ★ Tracing paper and pencil
- ★ Thin card for templates
- ★ Scissors
- ★ PVA glue and paintbrush, or hot-glue gun
- ★ Baker's twine or thin ribbon
- ★ Templates (see page 98)

STEP 1

Trace off the pennant template from page 98 and use it to cut out a template from thin card. Place the template on the back of your first piece of patterned paper and, with a pencil, draw on a few pennant shapes. The paper shown here is the reverse of a sheet of green, red and gold tartan paper.

STEP 2

Cut out your individual pennants with small, sharp craft scissors. Repeat steps 1 and 2 on all the pieces of patterned paper you want to use for your bunting until you have a good amount of pennants – this will depend on the length you want to create. Twenty-five pennants will make approximately 1m (39¼in) of bunting, not including any excess twine.

STEP 3
Arrange your pennants in an order you like.

STEP 4
Apply a little PVA glue near the top of each of the pennants. Place your twine carefully over the glue, remembering to leave some excess twine at each end for hanging up your bunting later. Once your pennants are completely dry, trim off the end of the twine.

Tip
You can leave your bunting single-sided if it's to go against a wall. If it's going to be seen from both sides, simply glue another pennant to each of the backs to sandwich in the twine.

Some more ideas for your mini bunting

Templates for the stockings, gold circles and star bunting can be found on page 98.

STOCKING BUNTING

We used a cheery blue spotted wrapping paper, teamed with a pink twine, for a fun, festive feel.

GOLD CIRCLES

Using glittered card is a great way of adding sparkle without the mess of loose glitter. Black and white twine gives the bunting a contemporary feel.

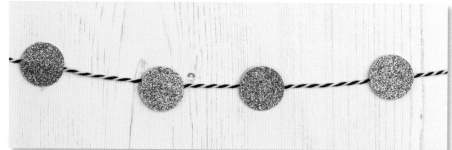

BLACK STARS

These stars can be used all year round – the neutral black makes them look modern and stylish. They could easily be made in gold, glittered or festive colours.

The finished swathes of bunting.

Use the star template to make little cake picks – simply attach them to cocktail sticks with glue, and use them to adorn your cakes.

Origami stars

Origami needn't be difficult. Often the finished creation can look almost impossible to achieve, but with a few simple steps you'll be making these beautiful stars in no time at all.

Once you've mastered the technique, you can create stars in a myriad different sizes – the small ones make wonderful tree decorations, and a large star makes for a very impressive alternative to a wreath.

You don't need to use origami papers to make these shapes, but the paper you use should be thin enough to fold easily.

You will need

★ Papers – enough to make fifteen squares at 70 x 70mm (2¾ x 2¾in) each.
★ Ruler
★ Scissors
★ Glue (not essential but will help stabilize your star)

To make one small star as below, cut fifteen 70 x 70mm (2¾ x 2¾in) paper squares.

STEP 1

Fold a square of paper corner to corner and press along the fold.

STEP 2

Open up the square. Turn it ninety degrees around and fold it corner to corner again.

STEP 3
Fold one corner to the centre of the square and press along the bottom fold.

STEP 4
Repeat step 3 to fold all four corners into the centre of the square.

STEP 5
Fold one outer edge in to meet the centre line and form half of a kite shape.

STEP 6
Fold in the opposite outer edge to complete the kite shape.

STEP 7

Turn the kite over and rotate it 180 degrees so that the long point is facing away from you. Fold the short point back on itself and press the fold.

STEP 8

Fold the shape in half vertically and press. This is one finished point of your star. When you tip the left edge of the point towards you, you should see two open slots.

STEP 9

Continue making the points of the star following steps 1–8. When you have fifteen points, slot them into one another – slot the front of one point into the slots on the back of another.

STEP 10

Fit the points together until you have a full star. To complete the origami star, use glue or sticky tape to secure the points in place.

Make... a star wreath

Our origami star can make a fabulous alternative to a traditional wreath. Simply use 150mm (6in) squares and follow the same steps to create a larger version of our decoration. You could hang it on the door, above the mantel, or use it as part of a table centrepiece.

Paper bird trims

Adorn your tree with these gorgeous little birds this Christmas! We have shown you how to make the partridge (the most complicated of the three) but you can find templates for all three birds – partridge, dove and robin – and their wings and tails on page 100.

We have made our birds look modern by going monochrome with a hint of colour; you could use multi-coloured, gold or silver papers, or opt for more realistic colours for your own birds.

You will need

* Thin card or watercolour paper
* Patterned paper or wrapping paper
* Tracing paper and pencil
* Thin card for template
* Small craft scissors
* Glue stick
* Black fineliner pen
* Black and white baker's twine
* Pink embroidery thread
* Sticky tape or washi tape
* Hole punch
* Templates (see page 100)

STEP 1
Trace the partridge body template, from page 100, onto thin card. Draw around the shape onto watercolour paper. Flip over the template and draw around it again to create the back of your bird.

STEP 2
Carefully cut out the two bird shapes using small craft scissors.

STEP 3
Cut two wings and four tail feathers from patterned paper, and use a hole punch to create circles for the eyes from the same paper.

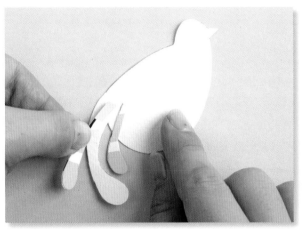

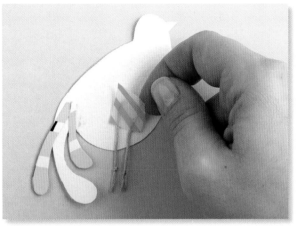

STEP 4

Glue the tail feather parts together by shape and size so they are patterned on both sides. Position the tail feathers on the reverse side of your first partridge cut-out, on either side of the bird's actual tail. Glue the tail feathers in place.

STEP 5

Cut a 80mm (3¼in) length of pink embroidery thread and make a knot at either end. Fold the length in half and secure it at the back of the bird with a piece of sticky tape – here we've used a scrap of colourful washi tape.

STEP 6

Stick the wing and the eye onto the front of your bird. Add details with a black fineliner pen: colour in the beak, draw on the eye, draw a design over the tail and add a few specks here and there for feather details.

STEP 7

Cut a 100mm (4in) length of twine, fold into a loop and secure at the back of the decorated half of your partridge with a piece of sticky tape or washi tape.

STEP 8

Finally, stick the front half of the partridge to the back half using a glue stick. Sandwich the twine between the two halves to secure it for hanging.

to...
Megan
.x.

Make... a paper bird gift tag

Our birds are very versatile. They can be used as all sorts of
decorations for Christmas. They are ideal for place names around
the Christmas table. You could hang them on the back of each
guest's chair; or, as shown here, they make the perfect gift tags for
your presents.

The completed paper bird trims.
Instead of adding loops to your birds, add lengths of twine and tie them to a twig to make a cute, festive bird mobile.

Winter tree domes

Create a stunning glittery forest display using glittered card and our templates, and house them under a glass dome sprinkled with snow.

Whether placed on the mantel, in a window or even as part of your Christmas table, this lovely little display will look very festive. You could even add a string of twinkly fairy lights inside for some added sparkle.

You will need

★ Glittered card in gold, silver, black and white
★ Glass dome or cloche with a base
★ Thin card for the templates
★ Tracing paper and pencil
★ Scissors
★ PVA glue and paintbrush
★ Artificial snow
★ Templates (see pages 99, 101 and 102)

You can use the steps for the winter tree dome to make a small decoration to hang on your tree. Simply trace and cut out the small, gold tree from page 99, plus two smaller trees (freehand) and stick them in place inside a shop-bought dome decoration. Fill the base with artificial snow, cover, then hang the decoration on your tree.

STEP 1

Trace off the five different-sized trees and the star from pages 99, 101 and 102 and use them to make templates from thin card.

STEP 2

• From gold glittered card: cut a large tree, a small tree and one star to go on the black glittered card tree.
• From silver glittered card: cut a medium tree.
• From white glittered card: cut a short, fat tree.
• From black glittered card: cut a medium, thin tree.

STEP 3

To make the trees sturdy, and so they look pretty from all angles, you will need to cut a second tree for each, so each tree has a pair. This time, flip over your tracing to create a mirror image so that when the trees are placed back to back they are symmetrical.

STEP 4

Glue the pairs of trees together, but only glue down part of the trunk. Snip off any excess card around the edges to neaten the tree up.

STEP 5

Fold out the base of the trunk to create two flat tabs.

Your five trees, ready to be placed in your dome!

Tip

You don't need to use glittered paper for this project. You could reuse some old scraps of wrapping paper or fabric swatches, sandwiching a piece of card in between to strengthen them.

STEP 6

Starting with the large gold tree, apply some glue to the tabs and position towards the back of the dome base – test putting the dome over the top to make sure the trees don't get knocked or squashed.

STEP 7

Add the trees in order: medium silver; short, fat white; medium, thin black; then the little gold tree. Glue the little gold star to the black tree. Remember to place the dome temporarily over the top of the arrangement to double-check the positioning of your trees.

STEP 8

Sprinkle some artificial snow around the base – you can add some little festive characters into the dome at this stage, too. Finally, place the glass dome over the top of the arrangement to complete your glittery forest display.

The completed winter tree dome.
Create a winter woodland display by adding some deer, miniature stars and a string of delicate fairy lights around your dome.

Folded-book angels

Upcycle your old books to create stunning and stylish paper angels. Simply by folding the pages of the book, adding a head and wings, you can transform your trash into treasure. You could add sparkle by dusting your angel with glitter and adding a face, keeping it Scandinavian-grey, or paint it minimalistic white like ours!

You will need

- ⭐ Old paperback book with at least 180 pages
- ⭐ Strong craft knife (optional)
- ⭐ Small felt pompom
- ⭐ Scissors
- ⭐ White spray paint
- ⭐ Newspaper
- ⭐ Hot-glue gun
- ⭐ PVA glue and paintbrush
- ⭐ Wing templates (see page 101)

STEP 1

Detach the cover of the book. Bend the book to make sure the glue of the spine is strong enough to withhold folding – you don't want the pages to fall out.

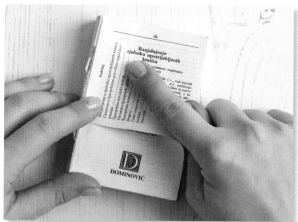

STEP 2

Starting with the first page, fold the top corner in to meet with the spine. Press along the fold.

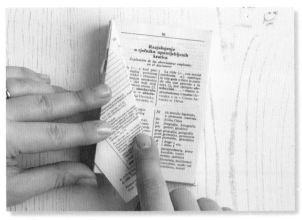

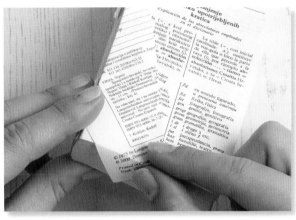

STEP 3

Fold the page over again to line up with the spine and press along the fold.

STEP 4

Fold the little triangle of overhanging paper down over the book block (the pages underneath) to make a crease line.

STEP 5

Tuck the triangle under the page at the crease line.

STEP 6

Fold the page down flat.

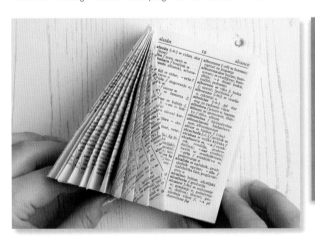

STEP 7

Repeat steps 2–6 on every page, flexing the spine as you go.

Tips

Depending on the type of book you're folding, the last pages can be quite difficult to get to – just keep flexing the spine.

You shouldn't need to glue any pages together, but if there is a gap at the back, apply some PVA glue to the last page and stick it to the first page.

STEP 8

Fold enough pages to form a full cone. You can then remove any excess pages by cutting through the spine with a craft knife.

STEP 9

Pick up your pompom and use a hot-glue gun to apply a little hot glue to your pompom.

STEP 10

Attach your pompom to the top of the book angel. Hold it for a few seconds to make sure it's adhered.

STEP 11

Trace off the wing templates from page 101 onto thin card. Draw around them onto two of the remaining pages of your old book, then cut them out. If your book pages are very thin, make two pairs of wings and stick them together to make two sturdier wings.

STEP 12

Glue the wings to your angel, slipping them between the pages to support them.

STEP 13

Place your angel on some protective newspaper. Working in a well-ventilated area, and following the manufacturer's instructions, shake up the can of spray paint and start applying bursts of paint from approximately 30cm (12in) away. The trick is to apply thin coats of paint rather than one thick layer. Wait for each coat to dry thoroughly before applying the next. Then allow your angel to dry completely before displaying him on a table, tray or window ledge!

Tip

We left some of the book visible to give it depth and interest, but you can paint yours completely if you wish.

Diamond decorations

These origami decorations are actually much easier to make than they look – once you've mastered the technique, you'll be making them with your eyes closed! These diamond decorations make a wonderful alternative to the traditional bauble, they are super stylish and you can make them in various sizes and from different-coloured papers to suit your decor.

You will need

⭐ Origami papers (or any thin paper): two shades, both 170 x 170mm (6¾ x 6¾in)
⭐ Scissors
⭐ PVA glue and paintbrush
⭐ Embroidery thread, baker's twine or thin ribbon
⭐ Cocktail stick

STEP 1
Take one square of paper. Fold it in half diagonally, corner to corner, then open it out again.

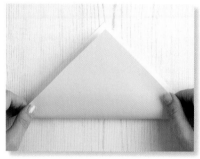

STEP 2
Fold the square diagonally in half the other way, this time keeping it folded.

STEP 3
With the base of the triangle towards you, take the right point up to the top point and fold.

STEP 4
Take the left point up to the top point, and fold.

STEP 5
Turn the diamond shape 180 degrees around so that the open end points towards you.

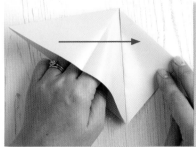

STEP 6
Open out the left side of the diamond.

STEP 7
Slide your fingers inside the left half of the diamond.

STEP 8
Push the left half of the diamond over towards the right edge.

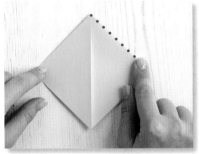

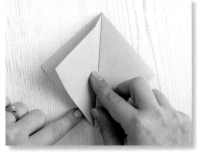

STEP 9
Press down along the crease.

STEP 10
Fold the right side – top flap only – back over to the left side of the diamond, as if turning a page.

STEP 11
Press down along the crease.

STEP 12
Repeat steps 7 to 11, this time starting from the right-hand side of the shape. Slide your fingers inside the right half of the diamond.

STEP 13
Push the right half over towards the left-hand edge.

STEP 14
Press down along the crease.

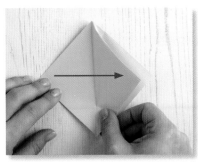

STEP 15

Repeat steps 12 to 14 starting from the left-hand side: fold the left side – top flap only – back over to the right side of the diamond. Press down along the crease.

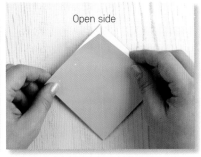

Open side

STEP 16

Turn the shape around so that the open side of the diamond is facing away from you.

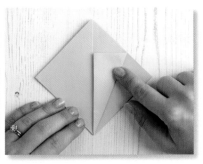

STEP 17

Fold the lower right side up and in towards the central crease.

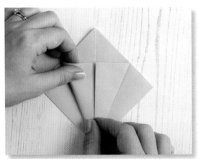

STEP 18

Repeat for the lower left side.

STEP 19

Flip over the shape.

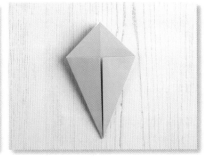

STEP 20

Repeat steps 17 and 18 on the reverse of the square. You will end up with a kite shape.

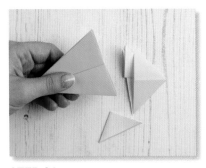

STEP 21

Cut off the excess triangles from the top.

STEP 22

The next three steps follow the same technique as you've used in steps 6–8. With the base of the triangle facing towards you, open out the left-hand section.

STEP 23

Open up the piece you have just folded out, and fold it over to the right...

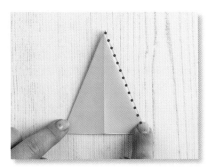

STEP 24
...then press along the crease.

STEP 25
Fold the right edge back across to the left.

STEP 26
Open up the right-hand section...

STEP 27
...then fold it up and over to the left edge again.

STEP 28
Flatten out the section then press down along the crease.

STEP 29
Fold the left edge back over towards the right.

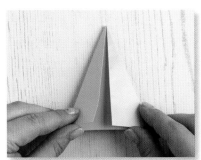

STEP 30
Turn the whole triangle over. Starting by folding the left edge back across to the right edge, repeat steps 22–29.

STEP 31
Once your whole piece is correctly folded, the base of your triangle should resemble a concertina, as above.

STEP 32

With the base of the triangle towards you, take the bottom-right corner and fold it up against the central crease.

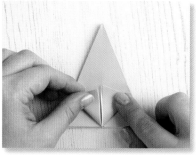

STEP 33

Fold the bottom-left corner up to the central crease in the same way.

STEP 34

Turn over your triangle and repeat steps 32 and 33 to fold up all the bottom corners on your shape in the same way. Open out your shape.

STEP 35

Fold the small triangles created from the folds in steps 28–29 inwards, and press the creases.

STEP 36

Repeat step 35 all the way around the shape, then place it to one side. Make an identical shape in a different colour, following steps 1 to 36.

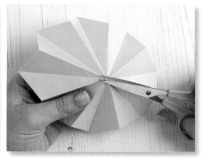

STEP 37

Snip a hole into the top of one of your origami shapes (this shape will form the top of your decoration).

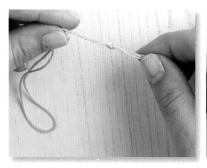

STEP 38

Cut a 300mm (11¾in) length of embroidery thread. Double it up and tie a knot in one end.

STEP 39

Feed the loop end of the thread up through the hole, using a cocktail stick to help push it through.

STEP 40

When the thread has been pulled all the way through, apply a dot of glue to the knot to secure it inside the shape.

STEP 41
Apply some glue to two of the points of your first paper shape. Take the second paper shape, line up the points and hold it in place until the glue secures.

STEP 42
Continue gluing around the edges, attaching two or three points at a time, until you have created one whole diamond. Leave to dry, then hang up your diamond decoration!

Tip
It's a good idea to work on gluing a few decorations at once, perhaps four or five — by the time you have glued a couple of sections of each of them, the first decoration will be strong enough to work on again.

The completed diamond decoration.
Group together a couple of diamond decorations and string them up with some festive foliage.

Tip
These decorations would look attractive hung up at a wedding, or for a baby shower, made up in pinks or blues (or yellows, greens or lilacs!).

Festive fun

Advent houses

Favour cones

Paper snowflakes

Wreath

Party hats

Advent houses

Make an Advent calendar you can bring out year after year and never get bored of. These tiny cardboard houses can be filled with sweet treats, a meaningful message or a keepsake – ring the changes with each tiny box. Whether hung from the tree, looped on some twine above a bed or lined up on a side table, they are sure to be a big hit with adults and children alike.

Above: a tall Advent house (a) and short Advent house (b).

The templates for more houses of different shapes and sizes can be found on pages 102–106.

You will need

★ Thin card in white, kraft (brown) and red – 297 x 210mm (11¾ x 8¼in)
★ Red and white paper
★ Tracing paper and pencil
★ Scrap card for templates
★ Ruler
★ Scissors
★ Craft knife
★ Cutting mat
★ Scoring tool
★ PVA glue and paintbrush

★ Hole punch
★ Baker's twine
★ Heart, star and circle paper punches
★ Cricut machine and mat (optional)
★ Rubber stamps – numbers, stars, anything Christmassy!
★ Black and red ink pads
★ Black fineliner pen
★ Decorative edging scissors
★ Templates (see pages 102–106)

House style

There are four styles of house, each slightly different. You can choose to incorporate all four and make six of each style plus a special house for 25th December. Or, if you prefer, you could follow just one or two of the designs – there is no wrong or right way.

Making the tall Advent house (a)

STEP 1
Trace the template from page 103 onto card. Next. draw around the template in pencil on thin kraft card.

STEP 2
Mark the score lines as dotted pencil lines, using a ruler.

STEP 3

Cut out the house – use large scissors to cut out the general shape of the house and smaller craft scissors to cut out the smaller details such as the underside flaps.

STEP 4

Use a ruler and a scoring tool to score along the marked lines. Set your house aside until step 7.

STEP 5

Punch out, or cut out (using a glue stick as a template) a 25mm (1in)-diameter circle from red paper.

STEP 6

Use a little number stamp dabbed in ink to stamp the circle.

STEP 7

Glue your numeral onto the front side of the house (with the largest flap). You can stick on a little punched-out heart or star as well if you'd like.

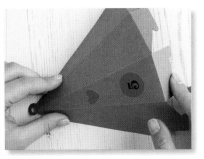

STEP 8

Punch or pierce a hole in the circle at the top of the house. Then, following the score lines, fold down the underside flaps, and fold in the scored edges.

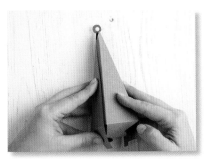

STEP 9

Fold the house together. This particular design does not require any glue – all the flaps slot together nicely.

STEP 10

Fold up the bottom flaps in the order shown above and slot them together. If you want to pop a little gift or message into your house, this is the stage at which to do it.

Making the short Advent house (b)

STEP 1

Trace the template from page 104 onto scrap card. Next. draw around it in pencil onto thin red card. Draw in the score lines as dotted pencil lines.

STEP 2

Cut out the house – use large scissors to cut out the general shape of the house and smaller craft scissors to cut out the smaller details. You could even cut out a window using a craft knife.

STEP 3

Use a ruler and a scoring tool to score along the marked lines.

STEP 4

Stick a thin, white-paper numeral onto what will be the front of the little house, as shown. We have used a Cricut machine to make the numeral but you can use a stamp or hand-draw the number and cut it out. Draw in a little window with black fineliner pen if you haven't already cut one out.

STEP 5

Cut or punch out two little white stars from the same paper (you can use the template on page 102) and stick these onto what will be the side walls of the little house.

STEP 6

Fold the scored flaps inwards and run glue along the flaps on the outside right edge of the house as shown above.

STEP 7
Fold the left edge around and stick it to the right edge.

STEP 8
Fold up the bottom flaps in the same order as for the tall Advent house as shown on page 73.

STEP 9
Trace off and cut out the roof template from page 102. Score down the centre, fold the roof in half and trim both edges with decorative edging scissors.

Tip
You don't have to add twine to all of your houses. Leave some of them plain so that they can sit on a surface.

STEP 10
Fold over the roof piece and punch a hole centrally through both halves at the top.

STEP 11
Thread a 200mm (7¾in) length of red and white baker's twine up through the two holes in the roof.

STEP 12
Apply some PVA to the top of the house. Position the roof in place, then press it down and smooth out any air bubbles. Set it aside to allow the roof to dry before you hang up your house.

Make... a tealight holder

Create a magical little tealight holder from one of the houses. Simply enlarge the house template on page 104 by 133% and construct it following the instructions on pages 74–75. Open up the bottom of the house and pop in an artificial tealight, making sure to switch it on before you put it in! *Voila*, a pretty little glowing house. You could create a whole miniature village of houses, each one with a battery-powered tealight inside.

Warning

Do not use a real flame tealight in your holder – this is a fire hazard and should not be attempted.

Opposite: a selection of Advent houses.

String up your Advent houses with washi tape and drape a twinkling string of fairy lights around them.

Favour cones

These cute little cones are ideal for hiding tiny goodies for your guests and are a contemporary alternative to traditional British Christmas crackers! These favour cones could be placed on the dinner table as a little welcome gift, or given to the kids as a special treat. They don't need to contain sweets – you could pop a special present inside. I've used pastel card, but you can use colours that suit your own Christmas colour scheme – sparkly metallics; pure, Scandinavian whites; or traditional greens and reds.

You will need

- ⭐ Four or five sheets of thin card in different colours – each 420 x 297mm (16½ x 11¾in)
- ⭐ Thin card for templates
- ⭐ Double-sided tape
- ⭐ Scissors
- ⭐ Small craft scissors
- ⭐ Pencil
- ⭐ Templates (see pages 107–109)

The finished size

The favour cone measures approximately 130mm (5in) tall by 80mm (3¼in) at its widest point.

STEP 1
Trace off the four favour cone templates on pages 107–109. Transfer these onto thin card and cut them out. Draw around each template onto different-coloured card.

STEP 2
Carefully cut out your four pieces. Use smaller scissors to cut the scalloped edges.

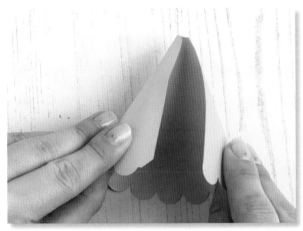

STEP 3

Curl up the card, so it gets used to the shape it will need to form.

STEP 4

Apply a strip of double-sided tape along one edge of the smallest cone piece so that it overlaps the edge. Cut the tape to half-width.

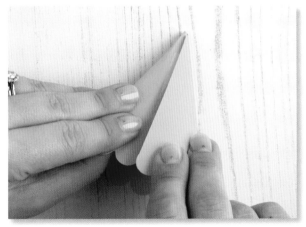

STEP 5

Remove the tape backing. Overlap the other edge of the card and hold it in place until the tape has adhered.

STEP 6

Make up the second-to-top section of your cone in the same way. Make sure that you wrap it tightly enough to fit inside the top cone piece.

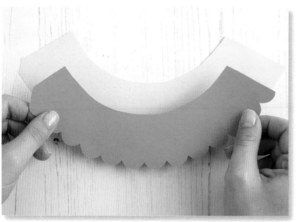

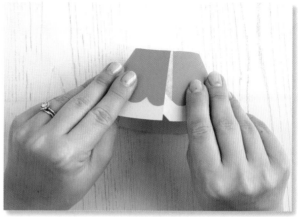

STEP 7

Glue the two lower sections together with their topmost curves lined up.

STEP 8

Once dry, curl the two lower sections round into shape, again using a half-width strip of tape to stick them together along one edge.

STEP 9

Once all four pieces have dried, you can stack them up!

The completed favour cones.
Fill your cones with colourful sweets!

Tip

As the cones don't have a base, place them on a plate or tray so they are easily moveable.

Paper snowflakes

When it comes to Christmas decorations, paper snowflakes are a classic, and a great craft to do with children, too. There are countless different designs you can create by simply snipping and cutting out various shapes from folded paper. As you experiment, you will discover which designs you find easy to achieve and which are more challenging.

A couple of sharp pairs of scissors (one small, one large) are essential for this project: trying to get through several layers of paper with blunt scissors is no fun! As you get more confident your designs will, no doubt, become more elaborate. You could try using larger sheets of paper for some wow-factor decorations, or create a very unique table runner, as we have overleaf.

Snowflake sizes

- **Large snowflake** – 400mm (15¾in)-diameter: use a 594 x 420mm (23½ x 16½in) sheet of paper.
- **Medium snowflake** – 300mm (11¾in)-diameter: use a 420 x 297mm (16½ x 11¾in) sheet of paper, as shown in the steps.
- **Small snowflakes**: make these from the offcuts of the large and medium snowflakes. They will be approximately 180mm (7in) and 120mm (4¾in) diameter.

You will need

- Good-quality white paper in various sizes (see right)
- Tracing paper and pencil
- Two pairs of sharp scissors, small and large
- Ruler
- Craft knife
- Cutting mat – optional
- Iron and tea towel
- PVA glue and paintbrush
- Templates (see page 110)

STEP 1
Take a sheet of paper 420 x 297mm (16½ x 11¾in). Pick up a corner of the paper and position it on the opposite edge of paper, lining up the edges to create a square.

STEP 2
Making sure the corner fold is neat and aligned, press along the diagonal fold. You can go over the fold with the handle of your scissors to make it crisp (see page 15).

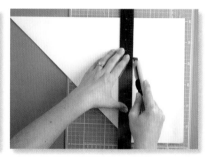

STEP 3
Cut off the excess freehand with scissors, or use a craft knife lined up against a long ruler to cut off the excess from the folded paper triangle. Put the excess aside to make a further two more small snowflakes later.

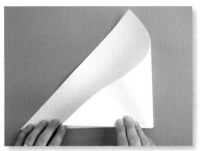

STEP 4

Lay your triangle on your work surface with the longest edge nearest to you. Fold the triangle in half, corner to corner, to make another triangle.

STEP 5

Rotate the triangle so that the straight edge is facing away from you. Then fold the triangle in half once more. Crisp the edge with your finger or with the handle of the scissors.

STEP 6

Open up the triangle again. With the point facing towards you, pick up the right-hand corner and fold it so that the long edge lines up with the central fold.

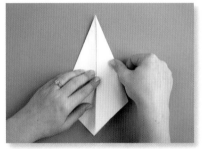

STEP 7

Repeat this process on the other side, so that you create a diamond shape. You may wish to rotate the shape 180 degrees to make it easier.

STEP 8

Fold the long right edge across to the long left edge to fold the diamond in half. Then press the fold to make it crisp.

STEP 9

There will be a straight edge, sandwiched in between the folds near the bottom of your shape. Fold the excess paper over this straight edge, to make a crease.

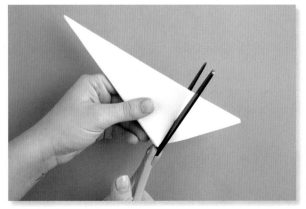

STEP 10

Use the crease as a guide to cut off the excess paper below. This is the starting point for all of our snowflakes.

Now comes the fun part – the designing! You can either copy the designs on page 110 by drawing them in pencil, freehand, onto your folded paper, or, if you're less confident, trace the templates onto the folded paper.

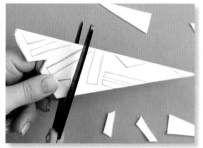

STEP 11

Draw, or trace, your chosen design onto the folded paper in pencil. You can shade the parts you'll be cutting out to make things easier.

STEP 12

Use large scissors to cut the straight lines, snipping off any large sections first.

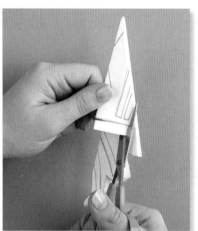

STEP 13

Use smaller scissors for the more intricate details, or where the paper is very thick. You can also use tweezers to help you remove these details (see page 14).

Tip

You can open up part of the snowflake and cut out individual details.

STEP 14

Once all the pieces have been cut out, carefully open out the snowflake, making sure not to tear it.

Tip

If you intend to make a runner, place your snowflakes along your table as you go, so you know how many more you need to make.

STEP 15

Place the snowflake under a tea towel and give it a good press on a medium heat to smooth out all the creases. Increase the heat if needed but be careful not to burn the paper.

STEP 16

Continue making up snowflakes of various sizes. Once you are happy with the amount and the arrangement, dab a spot of PVA glue underneath where one snowflake ends and another begins.

Below: an assembled paper snowflake table runner.

Wreath

Create a wreath that will potentially last a lifetime, simply by cutting leaves and berries from scraps of card or paper.

Our wreath is made up of traditional foliage shapes and colours – green holly, mistletoe and sprigs of red berries – but you could choose to go for rich jewel colours or even white and gold for a more contemporary result.

The rattan wreath.

You will need

- ⭐ 300mm (12in) rattan wreath (above, right)
- ⭐ Paper or thin card in a selection of greens, red and white
- ⭐ Tracing paper and pencil
- ⭐ Scissors
- ⭐ Scoring tool
- ⭐ Hot-glue gun, glue stick, or PVA glue and paintbrush
- ⭐ Cocktail stick
- ⭐ Hole punch
- ⭐ Cutting mat
- ⭐ Templates (see page 108)

Before you begin...

Trace the holly leaf, mistletoe and berry sprig templates from page 108. Transfer them onto thin card and cut them out to make your templates.

STEP 1
Draw round the holly templates onto the back of some green paper in one or two shades.

STEP 2
Repeat with the mistletoe template on light green paper.

STEP 3

Trace some berry sprigs onto red paper. The berries themselves are the holes – or chads – made by a standard office hole punch.

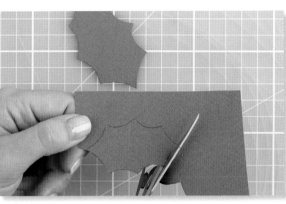

STEP 4

Cut out your holly leaves. To speed up the process, concertina the paper and cut out multiple leaves at once.

STEP 5

Score down the centre of each of the holly leaves.

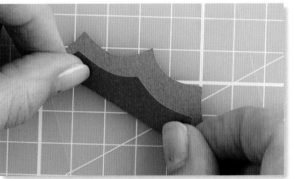

STEP 6

Fold the holly leaves inwards over the score line.

STEP 7

Apply a little PVA glue to the tips of the red sprigs. Use a cocktail stick as the sprigs are tiny.

STEP 8

Stick on the red berries (the hole punch chads) and leave them to dry.

STEP 9
Apply a little hot glue to the backs of the holly leaves and dot them around the rattan wreath.

STEP 10
Dot the mistletoe sprigs with hot glue. Intersperse the mistletoe among the leaves and leave to dry.

STEP 11
Finally, dot the berry sprigs with hot glue. Intersperse the berries around the wreath and leave to dry. Your wreath is now ready to hang up! Prop it on a shelf or a mantel or tie a length of ribbon to the rattan and hang your wreath on a door.

Make... a votive wrap

Working freehand, cut little leaves from deep-pink thin card or paper. Score each leaf. Apply a little PVA glue to the tips of some of the leaves and dip them into gold glitter. Tap off the excess and leave to dry. Glue the leaves to a 100mm (4in)-diameter rattan wreath. Finally, place a glass votive in the middle, pop in an artificial tealight and marvel at the magical twinkle as the light hits the glitter.

The completed wreath.
Hang your wreath above a mantel or shelf lined with gifts, foliage and candles.

Party hats

Be the life and soul of the party with these fun hats! Made from reinforced wrapping paper, it's an ideal project for using up pieces you have left over from Christmas. Paper sprays, flags and wool or felt pompoms are glued on top and ribbons added to complete the look. It's a great project to do with the kids in the lead-up to the New Year; this design can be used all year round for parties, too.

You will need

- ★ Wrapping paper
- ★ Thin card
- ★ Tracing paper and pencil
- ★ Scissors
- ★ Cutting mat
- ★ Scoring tool
- ★ Double-sided tape
- ★ Sticky tape or washi tape
- ★ Ribbon or leather twine
- ★ PVA glue and paintbrush
- ★ Cocktail sticks
- ★ Hot-glue gun
- ★ Peach crêpe paper or streamer
- ★ Wool or felt pompoms
- ★ Templates (see page 111)

Making the hat

STEP 1

Trace the hat template from page 111 twice (it is printed at half its actual width) using tracing paper and a pencil. Transfer your template onto a piece of thin card and also onto the reverse of your piece of wrapping paper. If the paper you are using is already sturdy enough you won't need to use cardboard inside the hat to support it.

STEP 2
Mark a score line to create a tab on one edge of the hat. Cut out both pieces.

STEP 3
Start curling the cardboard round, into the shape of the hat – this will help when constructing it later.

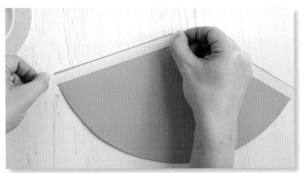

STEP 4
Cut two pieces of double sided tape, the length of the straight edges, and stick in place.

STEP 5
Peel off the backing from one of the strips of tape. Place the wrapping paper onto the tape, aligning the two short edges together.

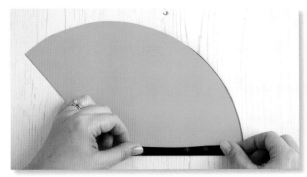

STEP 6
Peel off the second backing strip, curl the hat into shape and press down the wrapping paper onto the tape. Cut off any excess paper.

STEP 7
Fold along the scored edge to create a tab. Then apply another piece of double-sided tape along the length of the top side of the tab.

STEP 8

Peel off the backing, curl up the hat and overlap the two edges so the tape adheres to the underside.

STEP 9

Cut two 250mm (9¾in) lengths of ribbon or twine – such as the dark grey leather twine shown in the photograph above. Attach each length to the inside of the hat on opposite sides with a piece of sticky tape or washi tape.

Decorating the hat

Wool or felt pompom

STEP 1

Use a hot-glue gun to dab glue onto the pompom.

STEP 2

Attach the pompom to the top of your hat and leave to dry.

Paper spray

STEP 1
Cut four 150mm (6in) lengths from a 50mm (2in)-wide crêpe paper streamer, or four 150 x 50mm (6 x 2in) rectangles from a sheet of crêpe paper.

STEP 2
Cut strips approximately 5mm (¼in) apart, stopping about 10mm (½in) from the top of each of the four lengths. Don't worry – the cuts don't have to be precise.

STEP 3
Place the four fringed pieces on top of one another with the top edges lined up.

STEP 4
Begin to roll the pieces up tightly. Pinch the top-right edge between your thumb and forefinger and roll the paper inwards (from right to left).

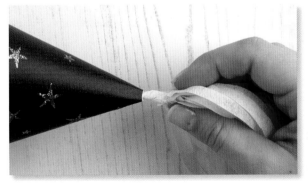

STEP 5
Feed the spray into the top of the hat and secure with sticky tape or PVA glue. Fluff up the paper spray.

Little flag

STEP 1

Draw around the little flag outline on page 111 onto the back of a piece of wrapping paper. Cut out the shape.

STEP 2

Place a cocktail stick in the centre of the flag and apply glue to the back of the flag. Fold the flag in half over the cocktail stick and press down to adhere the two sides together.

STEP 3

Pop the stick into the top of the hat and secure inside with sticky tape, making sure to cover over the sharp point of the stick.

Opposite: a selection of completed hats – ready to party!

Make... teeny-tiny party hats

Create miniature versions of our party hats to adorn little Christmas creatures!

Photocopy the hat template at 10% and trace the template onto the back of some wrapping paper and cut out. Apply a line of glue or a small piece of double-sided tape to one edge, wrap round and overlap so they stick together. Trim the hat down to the desired size for your animal. Apply a small blob of hot glue to the top of the hat and apply a small pompom. Then, either place the teeny-tiny hat on your animal, or use hot glue to keep it in place.

To make the miniature bunting, cut five 20mm (¾in) triangles from paper, apply some glue to the back of each and place a length of twine or embroidery thread into the glue. Once dry, tie each end to a bamboo stick, skewer or paper straw and trim off the excess.

Arrange the animals and bunting on top of a plain Christmas cake, and finally, dust the cake with icing sugar for a handmade feel.

Templates

All templates are reproduced at full size except where specified.

COLLAGED CHRISTMAS TREE CARD, PAGES 20–21

The numerical key shows you which of your decorative or plain papers can be used on each part of the tree.

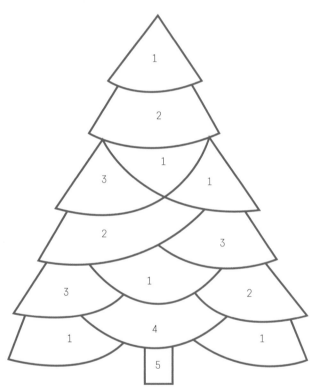

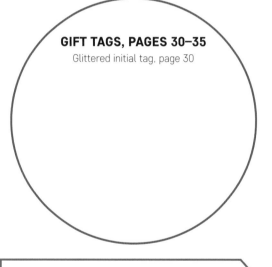

GIFT TAGS, PAGES 30–35

Glittered initial tag, page 30

GIFT TAGS, PAGES 30–35

Medium star, pages 31 and 32

GIFT TAGS, PAGES 30–35

Glittered, layered luggage tag, page 31

**PAPER FEATHER TAGS AND
GARLAND, PAGES 26–29**

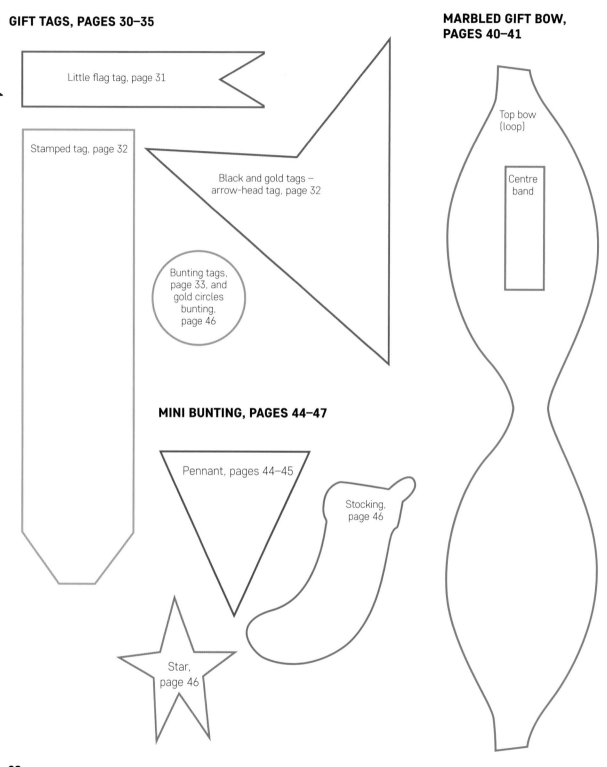

GIFT TAGS, PAGES 30–35

MARBLED GIFT BOW, PAGES 40–41

Little flag tag, page 31

Stamped tag, page 32

Black and gold tags – arrow-head tag, page 32

Bunting tags, page 33, and gold circles bunting, page 46

Top bow (loop)

Centre band

MINI BUNTING, PAGES 44–47

Pennant, pages 44–45

Stocking, page 46

Star, page 46

MARBLED GIFT BOW, PAGES 40–41

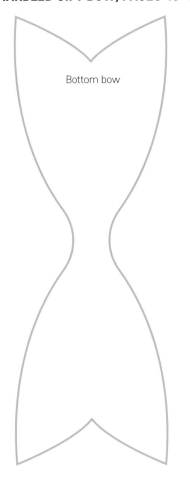

Bottom bow

EXTRA GIFT TAG TEMPLATES, PAGES 30–35

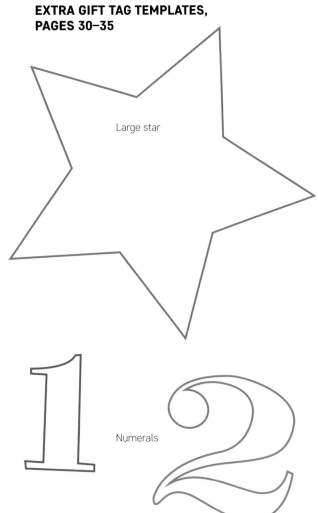

Large star

Numerals

WINTER TREE DOME, PAGES 56–59

Small gold glittered tree

**PAPER BIRD TRIMS,
PAGES 52–55**

Partridge tail feathers

Partridge body

Robin body

Robin chest

Dove body

Partridge wing

Robin wing

WINTER TREE DOME, PAGES 56–59

Gold star

White glittered tree

Black glittered tree

Silver glittered tree

FOLDED-BOOK ANGEL, PAGES 60–63

WINTER TREE DOME, PAGES 56–59

ADVENT HOUSES, PAGES 72–77

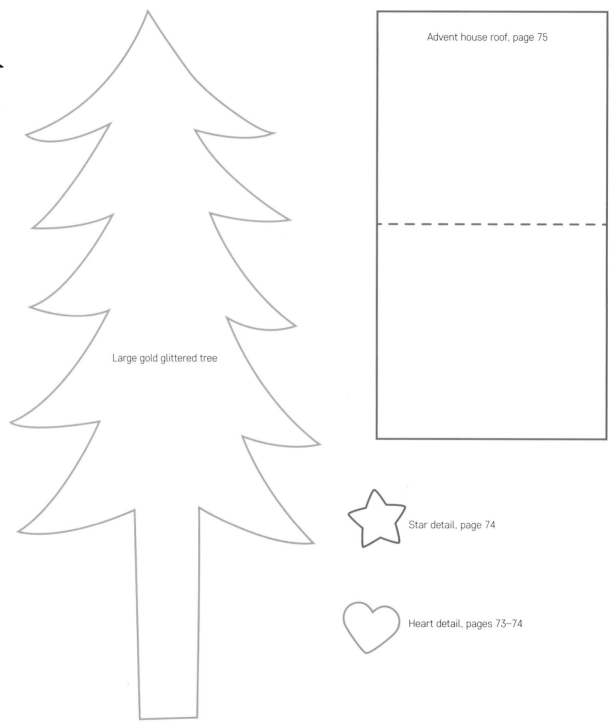

Advent house roof, page 75

Large gold glittered tree

Star detail, page 74

Heart detail, pages 73–74

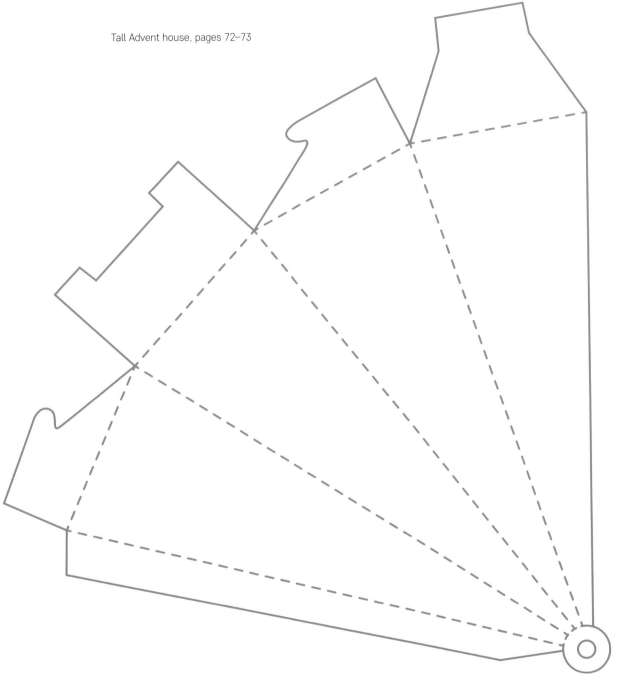

Tall Advent house, pages 72–73

**ADVENT HOUSES,
PAGES 72–77**

Templates

Short Advent house,
pages 74–75

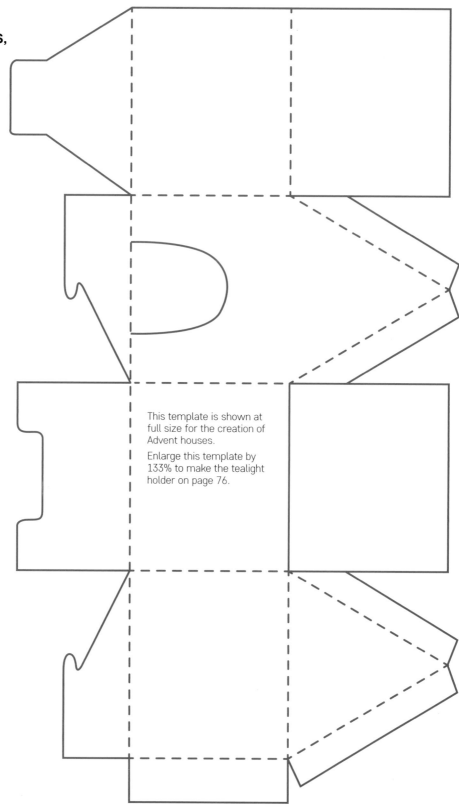

This template is shown at
full size for the creation of
Advent houses.

Enlarge this template by
133% to make the tealight
holder on page 76.

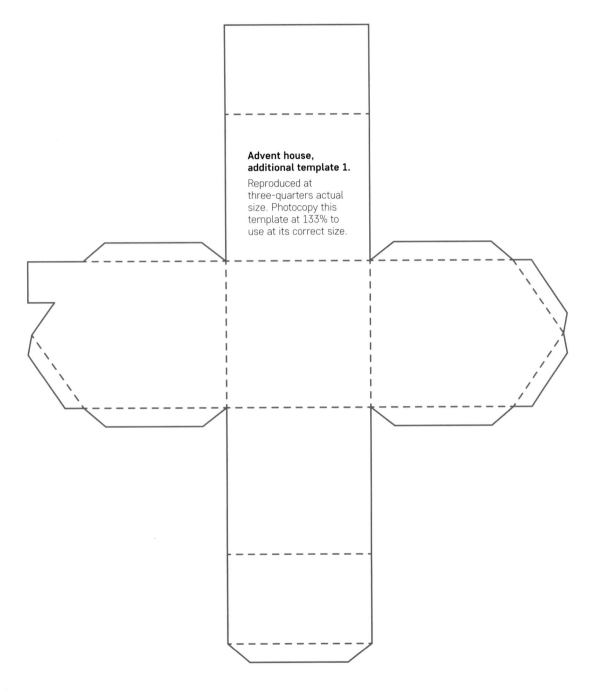

**Advent house,
additional template 1.**

Reproduced at
three-quarters actual
size. Photocopy this
template at 133% to
use at its correct size.

ADVENT HOUSES, PAGES 72–77

Advent house, additional template 2.

Reproduced at three-quarters actual size.
Photocopy this template at 133% to use
at its correct size.

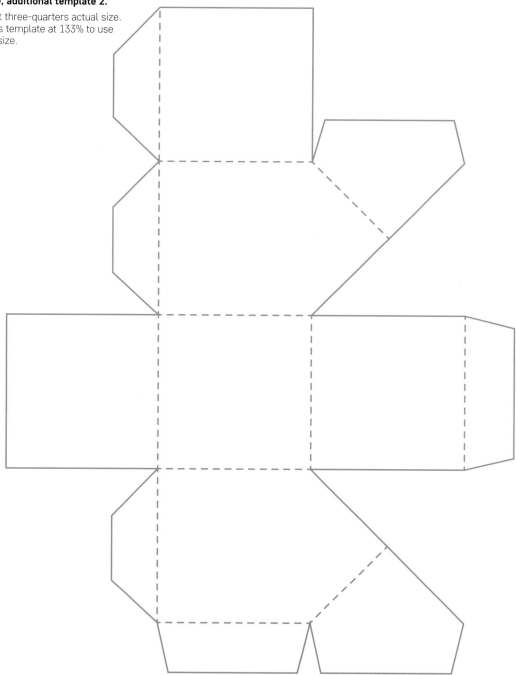

FAVOUR CONES, PAGES 78–81

Top layer

Second-to-top layer

**FAVOUR CONES,
PAGES 78–81**

WREATH, PAGES 86–89

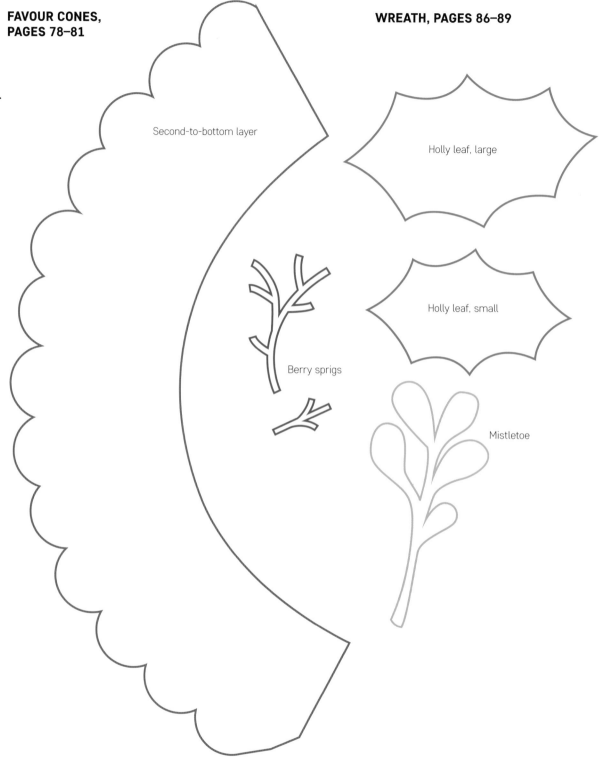

Second-to-bottom layer

Berry sprigs

Holly leaf, large

Holly leaf, small

Mistletoe

FAVOUR CONES, PAGES 78–81

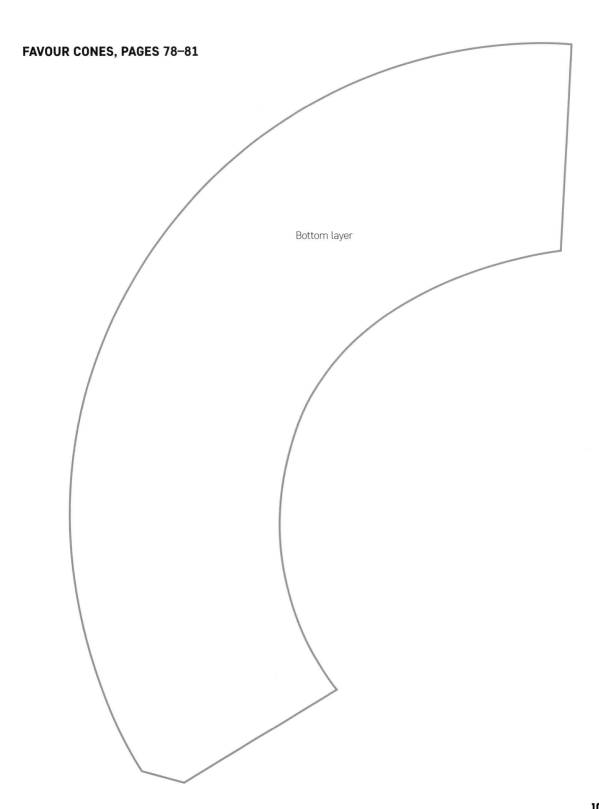

Bottom layer

PAPER SNOWFLAKES, PAGES 82–85

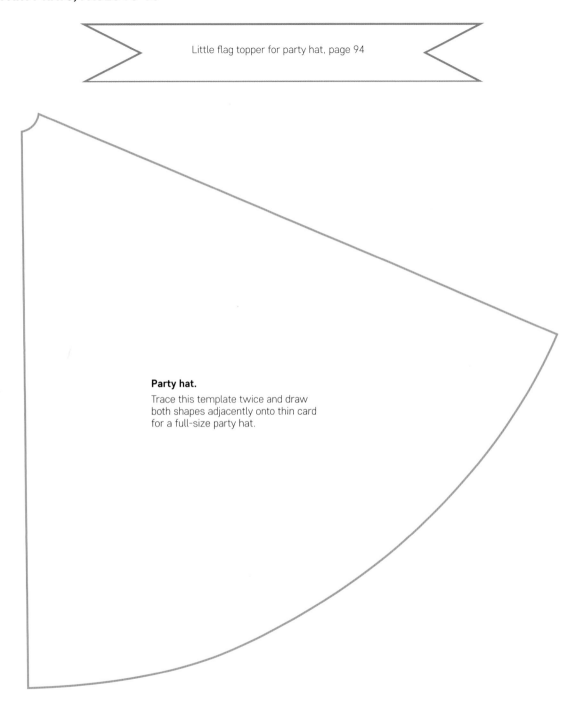

Little flag topper for party hat, page 94

Party hat.
Trace this template twice and draw both shapes adjacently onto thin card for a full-size party hat.

INDEX